A Gift for You

_____
Mom
TO

_____
Sue
FROM

_____
12/25/04
DATE

Prayers

AND

Promises

FOR

Women

Philis Boultinghouse

HOWARD
PUBLISHING CO.

Our purpose at Howard Publishing is to:

- *Increase faith* in the hearts of growing Christians
- *Inspire holiness* in the lives of believers
- *Instill hope* in the hearts of struggling people everywhere

Because He's coming again!

Prayers and Promises for Women © 2004 by Philis Boultinghouse
All rights reserved. Printed in the United States of America
Published by Howard Publishing Co., Inc.
3117 North 7th Street, West Monroe, LA 71291-2227
www.howardpublishing.com

04 05 06 07 08 09 10 11 12 13   10 9 8 7 6 5 4 3 2 1

Edited by Between the Lines
Cover design by LinDee Loveland & Stephanie D. Walker
Interior design by Stephanie D. Walker

Library of Congress Cataloging-in-Publication Data
Boultinghouse, Philis, 1951–
    Prayers and promises for women / Philis Boultinghouse.
        p. cm.
    ISBN: 1-58229-366-X
        1. Christian women—Prayer-books and devotions—English. I. Title.

BV283.W6B68 2004
242'.8431—dc22
                                                              2004042538

Scripture taken from the HOLY BIBLE, NEW INTERNATIONAL VERSION®. Copyright ©
1973, 1978, 1984 by International Bible Society. Used by permission of Zondervan. All rights
reserved.

Contents

*May my prayer be set before
you like incense; may the lifting
up of my hands be like the
evening sacrifice.*

PSALM 141:2

A Word to the Reader

Sometimes it feels as if the world demands that women be superheroes. When someone needs a hand, an answer, comfort, love, a meal, a smile, a lift, or a pat on the back, women feel the pressure to do, be, and know it all.

But what happens when the one who calms others' fears is afraid? What if the person with the answers has none? Just suppose the one others count on to keep things going feels tired, discouraged, or overwhelmed? Wise women know that although the demands may sometimes be too great, there's always someone they can turn to in prayer.

This unique book is filled with prayers from a woman like yourself and promises from the very best friend of all—your heavenly Father. You'll quickly identify with the prayers because they convey the needs, emotions, feelings, and struggles life presents to women on a regular basis. In the heavenly promises, you'll read personalized, paraphrased scriptures and experience the assuring presence and loving warmth only God's Word can give.

The encouragement that fills these heavenly promises will remain with you, inspire you, and fill you with hope. Let this little book bring you closer to heaven and offer words of encouragement that will impact your todays, tomorrows, and the rest of your life.

A Woman's Prayer

Dear God,

It's me—Your faraway child. A distance has been growing between us, and I'm not sure how to bridge the gap. I'm feeling disconnected from You, and I want to feel the strength and comfort of Your presence. I know in my head that You're out there and that You love me—I can almost see Your open arms extended to me. But my heart can't quite make the connection.

What makes it even worse is that I can't figure out what has created this distance between us. Maybe it's because I haven't spent much time with You lately; I've been preoccupied with work and my family . . . and with myself. Maybe it's because I've been working so hard at getting ahead in this world that I haven't set my sights on Your world. Maybe there's some sin in my heart that I haven't quite named.

Whatever it is, Lord, I want to find a way across this canyon between us. I want to know that I'm in Your presence and You're in mine.

Lord, clear a pathway before me that leads straight to You. I want to be with You, but I need Your help to find my way.

Your Faraway Child

A Heavenly Promise

Dearest Child,

It's good to hear from you. It's been quite a while since we've talked. But I've been here all along, and I've been waiting for you. When you call on Me, I will always listen. Of this you can be sure.

It pleases Me that you desire My presence. You may not know it, but you've already taken your first steps back to Me. Your faith that I exist and your earnest desire to seek Me will be rewarded. If you'll continue to seek Me with your heart and mind, you will find that I'm not far from you at all.

Lift your eyes toward heaven and take them off the things of the world. Seek the face of My Son. Fix your eyes on Him. When you do this, the path to Me will materialize before your feet.

Finally, My child, lift your heart to Me; open it and lay it bare. Expose and acknowledge the sin that builds a wall between us. When you do, I will run to embrace you. I will take you into My arms and welcome you with joy.

The gulf between us is disappearing as we speak. Welcome home.

Your Loving Father

from Hebrews 13:5; Jeremiah 29:12; Hebrews 11:6; Acts 17:27; Hebrews 12:2; Psalm 32:5; Luke 15:20–23

I Want to Be Closer to You
God's Word of Promise

He got up and went to his father.
"But while he was still a long
way off, his father saw him and was
filled with *compassion* for him;
he ran to his son, threw his arms
around him and *kissed* him."

LUKE 15:20

God has said, "Never will I leave you; never will I forsake you."

HEBREWS 13:5

THEN YOU WILL CALL UPON ME AND COME AND PRAY TO ME, AND I WILL LISTEN TO YOU.
JEREMIAH 29:12

Let us fix our eyes on Jesus, the author and perfecter of our faith, who for the joy set before him endured the cross, scorning its shame, and sat down at the right hand of the throne of God.

Hebrews 12:2

"You WILL SEEK ME AND FIND ME WHEN YOU seek ME WITH ALL YOUR HEART. I WILL BE found BY YOU," DECLARES THE LORD.
JEREMIAH 29:13–14

I acknowledged my sin to you and did not cover up my iniquity. I said, "I will confess my transgressions to the LORD"—and you forgave the guilt of my sin.

Psalm 32:5

• i want to be closer to you • i want to be closer to yo

Naught but God can
satisfy the soul.

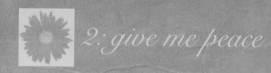

A Woman's Prayer

Dear Father,

I come to You needing Your calming peace. Lately my heart has been all tied up in knots, and my head has been full of worry. I don't know how long it's been since I've felt truly at peace. It's as if there's a huge boulder in my life, and it's my job to carry it. I've got it up on my shoulders, but I'm crushed by its weight, and I'm going nowhere.

The peace I once knew has left me, and it's been replaced by nagging worries and self-doubt. I've thought and thought about what I can do to fix this mess, but it seems to be out of my control. It's too big for me. I've prayed about it—oh, how I've prayed! But that big boulder is still up there.

This burden is with me in everything I do. I carry it with me everywhere I go. I can't get free of it. I long for Your peace. I ache for Your comfort. Fill me with Your peace, O Lord. Hold me in Your arms. Take this burden from me.

Your Fretful Child

A Heavenly Promise

Dear Fretful Child,

The burden you are trying to carry is not yours—it belongs to Me. Have I not told you to cast all your anxieties on Me? If you will throw your cares on Me, I will sustain you. I never let My righteous ones fall. If you will but let Me, I will remove the burden from your shoulders and set your hands free.

Though you have prayed about your worries, you have not left them at My feet. Every time you leave My throne room, you pick them back up and take them with you. Instead of trying to figure this out on your own, trust in Me with all your heart. If you will acknowledge Me and My power, I will make your paths straight.

Redirect your worries into fervent prayer. Pour out your heart to Me, for I am your God of refuge. Bring everything to Me—all your requests and petitions, and bring some thanks too. If you will substitute prayer for anxiety, you'll find that My peace will fill your heart and mind.

Whatever troubles you, look to Me and know that I will rescue you. I have never forsaken those who seek Me.

Your God of Rescue

from 1 Peter 5:6–7; Psalms 55:22; 81:6–7; Proverbs 3:5–6
Psalm 62:8; Philippians 4:6–7; Psalm 9:10

Give Me Peace
God's Word of Promise

Do not be anxious about anything,
but in everything, by *prayer*
and petition, with thanksgiving,
present your requests to God.
And the *peace* of God,
which transcends all understanding,
will guard your *hearts* and
your minds in Christ Jesus.

PHILIPPIANS 4:6–7

Cast your cares on the LORD and he will sustain you; he will never let the righteous fall.

PSALM 55:22

TRUST IN HIM AT ALL TIMES, O PEOPLE; POUR OUT YOUR HEARTS TO HIM, FOR GOD IS OUR REFUGE.

PSALM 62:8

I removed the burden from their shoulders; their hands were set free from the basket. In your distress you called and I rescued you.

Psalm 81:6–7

Trust IN THE LORD WITH ALL YOUR *heart* AND LEAN NOT ON YOUR OWN UNDERSTANDING; IN ALL YOUR WAYS *acknowledge* HIM, AND HE WILL MAKE YOUR PATHS *straight*.

PROVERBS 3:5–6

Those who know your name will trust in you, for you, LORD, have never forsaken those who seek you.

Psalm 9:10

*Worry gives
a small thing
a big shadow.*

SWEDISH PROVERB

A Woman's Prayer

Dear God of Love,

I've read in the Bible that You want me to love others—all others. Yet there's one particular person—You know who I mean—whom I just can't stand to be around.

This person rubs me wrong in every way possible. Every time I think about this person, I feel agitated and angry, and I start turning over in my mind all the little things about this person that bother me. My thoughts, feelings, and emotions—even my relationship with You—have been affected.

And I hate to admit it, but part of me doesn't want to let go of this dislike. Yet I know that You love me—with all my faults, with all my shortcomings—and that You want me to love others.

The fact that your Word commands me to love others makes me think it must be something I can *choose* to do. But I'm stuck; I don't know how to will that feeling into being.

So I was thinking . . . since You created this world out of nothing, can You create love in me where none exists? I want to please You, and I want my heart to be right. I need Your love in me.

Your Child Who Needs Love

A Heavenly Promise

Dear Child,

I *can* create love in you—all I need is a willing heart. Your coming to Me shows that you have such a heart. And because your heart is responsive to me, I have heard you. You're right to note that love is a commandment. Because love is central to who I am, it must be central to who you are as My child.

Concentrate first on changing your actions and thoughts. Your heart will follow. Let Me tell you how love acts and thinks: Love is patient and kind. It's protective, trusting, and hopeful. Love is not envious or boastful or proud. It is not rude or self-seeking. It's not easily angered, nor does it keep a record of wrongs.

Live out My definition of love. Do something kind for the person you dislike; check your heart to see if you are envious. Obey Me in how you treat this person, and you will find that obedience and a change of heart go hand in hand. As you invest yourself and your time into improving this relationship, I will give you a new heart and put a new spirit in you. I will replace your heart of stone with a heart of flesh.

Your God of Love

from 2 Kings 22:19; John 15:12; 1 John 3:11; 4:8; 3:18; 1 Corinthians 13:4–7; 1 Kings 8:61; Psalm 119:112; Deuteronomy 30:10, 6, 14; Ezekiel 36:26; Luke 12:34

I Need Your Love in Me
God's Word of Promise

Love is *patient*, love is kind.
It does not envy, it does not boast,
it is not proud. It is not rude,
it is not *self-seeking*, it is not
easily angered, it keeps no record
of wrongs. Love does not delight
in evil but *rejoices* with the truth.
It always protects, always trusts,
always hopes, always *perseveres*.

1 CORINTHIANS 13:4–7

My command is this: Love each other as I have loved you.

JOHN 15:12

BECAUSE YOUR HEART WAS RESPONSIVE AND YOU HUMBLED YOURSELF BEFORE THE LORD . . . I HAVE HEARD YOU, DECLARES THE LORD.

2 KINGS 22:19

Whoever does not love does not know God, because God is love.

1 John 4:8

Obey THE LORD YOUR GOD AND KEEP HIS *commands* AND DECREES THAT ARE WRITTEN IN THIS BOOK OF THE LAW AND TURN TO THE LORD YOUR GOD WITH ALL YOUR *heart* AND WITH ALL YOUR SOUL.

DEUTERONOMY 30:10

Where your treasure is, there your heart will be also.

Luke 12:34

Your hearts must be fully committed to the LORD our God, to live by his decrees and obey his commands.

1 Kings 8:61

*With the knowledge
of God comes love.*

CATHERINE OF SIENA

A Woman's Prayer

Dear Lord,

For a long time I've told myself *That's just the way I am.* Some people are timid and shy; some are outgoing and expressive; I'm just up-front and honest about my feelings—if something makes me mad, I don't hold it in. I tell people exactly what I think and how I feel. If they don't like it, that's tough—it's just the way I am.

But lately Your Spirit has been convicting me, Lord, and I'm beginning to see that You want me to be more than "the way I am." I'm beginning to see that You continually call me higher—to be more than who I am naturally.

Still, knowing I need to control my temper is not the same thing as doing it. Each day I wake up determined to do better, but by the end of the day, I've blown it by blowing up. I can see, now, how my words and harshness hurt people; I just don't know if I'm going to be able to change. Each failure brings another dose of discouragement. Is there any hope for change in me?

Can You help me, Lord?

Your Hot-Tempered Child

A Heavenly Promise

Dear Beloved,

There is hope! The same power I exerted to raise My Son from the dead is available for all who believe. It's available to you.

When people do things that irritate you—and there's no doubt they will—don't respond out of anger or in haste. Hold your tongue and take time to think. The more you say when you're angry, the more likely you are to say something you shouldn't. And when you can go beyond merely holding your tongue and actually choose to overlook the offense, you show your wisdom by your patience. If you can learn to put your own feelings aside and consider what's best for the other person, you will be one step closer to being like My Son.

Keep close watch over your words, and keep your anger under control. You'll find that a quiet word from you will often calm the anger of others as well as your own.

Keep this guideline close to your heart at all times: "Be quick to listen, slow to speak and slow to become angry." You can change. I'm in the business of making old things new.

Your Dynamic God of Change

from Ephesians 1:18–20; Romans 3:23; Proverbs 29:11; 10:19; 19:11; Philippians 2:3–4; Proverbs 16:23; 15:1; James 1:19; 2 Corinthians 5:17

Cool My Temper
God's Word of Promise

I pray also that the eyes of your
heart may be *enlightened* in order
that you may know the hope
to which he has called you, the
riches of his glorious *inheritance* in
the saints, and his incomparably
great *power* for us who believe.

EPHESIANS 1:18–19

A fool gives full vent to his anger, but a wise man keeps himself under control.

PROVERBS 29:11

A MAN'S WISDOM GIVES HIM PATIENCE; IT IS TO HIS GLORY TO OVERLOOK AN OFFENSE.

PROVERBS 19:11

If anyone is in Christ, he is a new creation; the old has gone, the new has come!

2 Corinthians 5:17

Each OF YOU SHOULD LOOK NOT ONLY TO YOUR OWN *interests*, BUT ALSO TO THE INTERESTS OF *others*.

PHILIPPIANS 2:4

My dear brothers, take note of this: Everyone should be quick to listen, slow to speak and slow to become angry.

James 1:19

A gentle answer turns away wrath, but a harsh word stirs up anger.

Proverbs 15:1

• cool my temper • cool my temper • cool my tem

*People who fly into a rage
always make a bad landing.*

WILL ROGERS

A Woman's Prayer

Dear Lord,

I'm embarrassed at my weakness and troubled by my lack of faith. I believe in You, but sometimes my shield of faith falls, and I'm blindsided by Satan's flaming arrows of doubt. I remind myself of the father who asked Jesus to heal his son: "I believe, help my unbelief."

I struggle when things don't turn out like I'd expected—especially when I've prayed about them. I struggle when someone I love is hurting. I struggle when someone I love is hurting me. I struggle when my personal growth is slow, when the things that have plagued me for years still trip me up.

When I'm bombarded with difficulties, my faith wavers; and in my self-pity, I doubt Your love—especially when the really big hurts come.

Right now, Lord, I need to hear Your words of encouragement; I need to know You're near, that You are at work in my life. I need to know that You see the doubt in my heart yet still love me and won't reject me. As Jesus answered the doubting father, I hear Jesus' words in my heart: "Anything is possible to those who believe." I believe, Lord—help my unbelief.

Your Doubting Child

A Heavenly Promise

Dear Doubting Child,

Your quest for increased faith pleases Me. Be encouraged to know that I will reward you for your efforts to seek Me.

Understand that faith doesn't begin with you. The source of faith is My Son. He is the author and perfecter of your faith. As you fix your eyes on Him, your faith will grow.

Remember past times that I've helped you. Think on the ways I've helped others you know; look in My Word and see that I've always taken care of those who follow Me.

Life is difficult at times; things don't always turn out as you desire. But know this: I take all the events of your life—good and bad—and weave them together for your ultimate good. The tough times actually serve to polish and refine you until you have the purity and shine of the finest gold.

No matter what happens, remember that I am a God of power. Nothing is impossible with Me. I'm also a God of hope, and I'll fill you with joy and peace as you trust in Me. Trust Me with all your heart; acknowledge Me in all you do, and I will make all your paths straight.

Your Faithful God

from Hebrews 11:6; 12:2; Deuteronomy 32:7; Psalm 105:5; 1 Peter 1:6–7; Luke 1:37; Romans 15:13; Proverbs 3:5–6

Increase My Faith
God's Word of Promise

Rejoice, though now for a little while you may have had to suffer grief in all kinds of trials. These have come so that your *faith*—of greater worth than gold, which perishes even though refined by fire—may be proved *genuine* and may result in praise, glory and honor when Jesus Christ is revealed.

1 PETER 1:6–7

30

*W*ithout faith it is impossible to please God, because anyone who comes to him must believe that he exists and that he rewards those who earnestly seek him.

HEBREWS 11:6

LET US FIX OUR EYES ON JESUS, THE AUTHOR AND PERFECTER OF OUR FAITH.

HEBREWS 12:2

Remember the wonders he has done, his miracles, and the judgments he pronounced.

Psalm 105:5

Nothing IS IMPOSSIBLE WITH GOD.

LUKE 1:37

May the God of hope fill you with all joy and peace as you trust in him, so that you may overflow with hope by the power of the Holy Spirit.

Romans 15:13

31

• increase my faith • increase my faith • increase my fa

*Faith is the daring of
the soul to go farther
than it can see.*

WILLIAM NEWTON CLARKE

6: help me not to fear

A Woman's Prayer

Dear Heavenly Father,

I come to You hoping You can help me overcome a growing problem. Lately I've felt a menacing presence, an overwhelming uneasiness in my life. And I've finally figured out what it is. It's fear. I'm not sure when it started or why, but it's getting stronger, and I'm getting weaker.

I've been trying to figure out what I'm afraid of. It's a lot of things. I'm afraid of not measuring up, afraid of making mistakes, afraid of what the future holds, afraid of letting my loved ones down—afraid of letting You down.

I know You've called me to trust You and that You've commissioned me to live boldly. I want to be brave; I want to live fearlessly—but I need Your help. Lord, instill in me Your courage, for I have none of my own. Fill me with Your fortitude, for I'm weak. Infuse me with the conviction that I can do all things with Your help. Train my heart to be brave.

Please take the fear from my heart and replace it with confidence and courage to live the life You've called me to.

Fearfully Yours

A Heavenly Promise

Dearest Child of Mine,

Come to Me, for I want to gather you in My arms and carry you close to My heart. The world is a frightening place—for it is fallen and under the control of the evil one—but fear has no place in the hearts of My children. Fear is from the evil one, and he uses it to cloud your view of My face. The only way to combat your fear is by trusting Me.

I haven't given you a spirit of timidity and fear. Rather, I've given you a spirit of power, love, and self-discipline. Because you are My child, you already have overcome the forces of this world; for I am in you, and I am greater than the prince of this world. As long as I'm beside you, you need not fear, for I will help you. I will never forsake you.

Stand firm in your faith. Don't be afraid or discouraged. When fear does grip your heart, fix your eyes on My Son and continue to live the life I've set before you. Don't be distracted by the battle around you; for the battle is not yours but Mine, and I will fight it for you.

Your God of Strength

from Isaiah 40:11; 1 John 5:19; John 14:1; 2 Timothy 1:7; 1 John 5:4; 4:4; Romans 8:32; Deuteronomy 31:8; 1 Corinthians 16:13; Hebrews 12:1–2; 2 Chronicles 20:15

Help Me Not to Fear
God's Word of Promise

The LORD himself goes *before* you
and will be with you; he will never
leave you nor *forsake* you. Do not be
afraid; do not be discouraged.

DEUTERONOMY 31:8

He tends his flock like a shepherd: He gathers the lambs in his arms and carries them close to his heart; he gently leads those that have young.

ISAIAH 40:11

GOD DID NOT GIVE US A SPIRIT OF TIMIDITY, BUT A SPIRIT OF POWER, OF LOVE AND OF SELF-DISCIPLINE.

2 TIMOTHY 1:7

Everyone born of God overcomes the world. This is the victory that has overcome the world, even our faith.

1 John 5:4

Be ON YOUR GUARD; STAND FIRM IN THE FAITH; BE MEN OF *courage*; BE STRONG.

1 CORINTHIANS 16:13

He who did not spare his own Son, but gave him up for us all—how will he not also, along with him, graciously give us all things?

Romans 8:32

• help me not to fear • help me not to fear • help m

Only he who can say,
"The Lord is the strength
of my life," can say, "Of
whom shall I be afraid?"

ALEXANDER MACLAREN

A Woman's Prayer

Dear God in Heaven,

I come to You with my heart in my hands. My heart's desire, Father, is to please You—to live a life You can be proud of. Your Word speaks of living a life worthy of my calling, and that's what I want to do.

Yet I fail You every single day, and I am so far from who You want me to be. I'm easily distracted by the things of this world, and it doesn't take much to pull my focus from You and onto the problems in my life.

But, Father, I'm willing to be shaped and molded by You. I want to be a source of blessing and encouragement to others. I want to be an instrument in Your mighty hands. I want to be Your hands, Your feet, and Your arms in this world.

Yet I'm weak, and I've failed many times. Is my life one that You can use? I want to be worthy of Your call.

Your Willing but Weak Servant

A Heavenly Promise

Dear Servant Child,

Be confident that the good work I began in you will be carried to completion, for I'm continually at work in you. Just as a potter gives shape to clay, so will I shape you to bring about My will.

The weakness you see in yourself actually works to My advantage, for My power is most effective in your weakness. In fact, the power of Christ rests on you when you're weak. I have chosen to use what this world sees as foolishness and weakness to shame the "wise" and the "strong."

Be assured that I, the God who brought Jesus back from the dead, will equip you with everything you need for doing My will. You are My workmanship—created for doing good works. I prepared good things for you to do before you were even born. And now I will empower you to fulfill your good intentions and to live out your actions prompted by faith.

I encourage you not to neglect the special gifts I've placed within you but to fan them into flame. Use them to administer My grace. My Word instructs you how to please Me—and this you are doing. I urge you to do it more and more.

Your Equipping Father
from Philippians 1:6; 2:13; Jeremiah 18:6; Isaiah 64:8; 2 Corinthians 12:9–10; 1 Corinthians 1:27; Hebrews 13:20–21; Ephesians 2:10; 2 Thessalonians 1:11–12; 1 Timothy 4:14; 2 Timothy 1:6; 1 Peter 4:10; 1 Thessalonians 4:1

I Want to Be Your Instrument
God's Word of Promise

May the God of peace, who
through the *blood* of the eternal
covenant brought back from the
dead our *Lord Jesus*, that great
Shepherd of the sheep, equip you
with *everything* good for doing
his will, and may he work in us
what is *pleasing* to him, through
Jesus Christ, to whom be glory
for ever and ever.

HEBREWS 13:20–21

42

$\mathscr{I}$t is God who works in you to will and to act according to his good purpose.

PHILIPPIANS 2:13

LIKE CLAY IN
THE HAND OF
THE POTTER,
SO ARE YOU IN
MY HAND.
  JEREMIAH 18:6

God chose the weak things of the world to shame the strong.
  1 Corinthians 1:27

*W*e ARE GOD'S WORKMANSHIP, CREATED IN CHRIST JESUS TO DO GOOD WORKS, WHICH GOD *prepared* IN ADVANCE FOR US TO DO.
  EPHESIANS 2:10

Each one should use whatever gift he has received to serve others, faithfully administering God's grace in its various forms.
  1 Peter 4:10

WE CONSTANTLY PRAY FOR YOU, THAT OUR GOD MAY COUNT YOU WORTHY OF HIS CALLING, AND THAT BY HIS POWER HE MAY FULFILL EVERY GOOD PURPOSE OF YOURS AND EVERY ACT PROMPTED BY YOUR FAITH.
  2 THESSALONIANS 1:11

Fan into flame the gift of God, which is in you.
  2 Timothy 1:6

God is the organist, we are
his instrument,
His Spirit sounds each pipe and
gives the tone its strength.

ANGELUS SILESIUS

• i want to be your instrument • i want to be

A Woman's Prayer

Dear God,

I don't mean to sound ungrateful, but how long must I wait before You answer my prayer? I've come to You over and over on this matter, but nothing seems to change. I see others around me having their requests answered, yet here I sit in the same predicament.

Have I done something to offend You? Are You ignoring me to punish me? It feels as if You're hiding Your face from me or as though my prayers reach the ceiling of my house and go no farther. Every day, thoughts of defeat plague me, and my heart is full of sorrow. I know You have the power to act on my behalf. I don't understand why You're taking so long.

I need to know that You hear me. I need to know You care. Are You listening?

Waiting on You

A Heavenly Promise

Dear Child,

Let me assure you, my weary daughter, that My eyes are on you and that My ears are attentive to your prayer. Be brave and courageous as you wait on Me, for I will never forsake you. Even if you don't understand My timing or My answer, know that My ways are perfect and just. I am good to those who seek Me and whose hope is in Me. It is good to wait quietly for My salvation.

No matter what you're going through, nothing can separate you from My love. If you maintain your hope in Me, I will renew your strength. You will soar on wings like eagles; you'll run and not grow weary; you'll walk and not faint.

Take heart, be strong, and wait for Me as a watchman waits for the light of dawn. Be assured that I long to be gracious to you; that I get off My throne and on My feet to show compassion to you. Watch in hope for My hand to move on your behalf; wait for Me and know that I hear you. While you wait, be encouraged by the assurance of My love.

Worth the Wait

from 1 Peter 3:12; Deuteronomy 31:6; 32:4; Lamentations 3:24–26; Romans 8:38–39; Isaiah 40:31; Psalms 27:14; 130:6; Isaiah 30:18; Micah 7:7; Jude 21

Please Answer Me
God's Word of Promise

Neither death nor *life*, neither
angels nor demons, neither the
present nor the future, nor any
powers, neither height nor depth, nor
anything else in all *creation*, will be
able to separate us from the love of
God that is in *Christ Jesus* our Lord.

ROMANS 8:38–39

The eyes of the Lord are on the righteous and his ears are attentive to their prayer.

1 PETER 3:12

HE IS THE ROCK, HIS WORKS ARE PERFECT, AND ALL HIS WAYS ARE JUST. A FAITHFUL GOD WHO DOES NO WRONG, UPRIGHT AND JUST IS HE.

DEUTERONOMY 32:4

I say to myself, "The LORD is my portion; therefore I will wait for him." The LORD is good to those whose hope is in him, to the one who seeks him; it is good to wait quietly for the salvation of the LORD.

Lamentations 3:24–26

Those WHO HOPE IN THE LORD WILL *renew* THEIR STRENGTH. THEY WILL SOAR ON WINGS LIKE EAGLES; THEY WILL *run* AND NOT GROW WEARY, THEY WILL *walk* AND NOT BE FAINT.

ISAIAH 40:31

My soul waits for the Lord more than watchmen wait for the morning.

Psalm 130:6

• please answer me • please answer me • please answer

We do not obtain the most
precious gifts by going
in search of them but by
waiting for them.

SIMONE WEIL

A Woman's Prayer

Dear Lord of Heaven,

I'm coming to You with a hunger in my heart and a longing in my soul. What I'm wanting is more of You in me.

You are so high above me, so lofty and majestic. Is it possible that I, a human, could have a real relationship with You? I go to church, I pray, I try to live right and be kind; but it's You I'm wanting more of. I want to be aware of Your presence throughout my day. I want to be guided by Your hand continually.

During the fleeting moments when I *am* aware of Your presence in me, I'm filled with a sense of peace and purpose. I want more of this. I want to go deeper into You.

I want the essence of me to be You. I want to be defined by You, and I want that definition to define who I am to others. Fill me with Your presence, Lord—so full that there's no room for me. And as I become filled with You, let me overflow in acts of kindness, wisdom, unselfishness, and love for others.

Is what I desire even possible? Do You desire this intimacy with me?

Wanting You

A Heavenly Promise

Dear Seeking Child,

I will be found by you! In fact, I'm continually on the look-out for those who are looking for Me. When you seek Me with all your heart, you'll find Me. As you come near to Me, I'll respond by coming near to you. I'm near to all who call Me.

You'll find intimacy with Me as you humble yourself, pray, and seek My face. My heart yearns for relationship with you as a father yearns for relationship with his child. And like a mother hen desires to gather her chicks under her wing, I desire to gather you to Me. I delight in you.

The way to lose yourself in Me is to die to yourself—just as Christ died for you—then My Son will live in you, and you will be filled with Him. As Christ dwells in your heart, My fullness will live in you also. And the fuller you are of Me, the more My goodness will spill over into the lives of others as you exercise the gifts I've given you.

Your God of Love

from Psalms 9:10; 14:2; Jeremiah 29:13–14; James 4:8; Psalm 145:18; 2 Chronicles 7:14; 1 Chronicles 16:10–11; Matthew 23:37; Jeremiah 31:20; Galatians 2:20; Colossians 2:9–10; Ephesians 3:16–19; 4:11–13

Take Me Deeper into You
God's Word of Promise

I pray that out of his glorious riches he may *strengthen* you with power through his Spirit in your inner being, so that Christ may *dwell* in your hearts through faith. And I pray that you, being rooted and established in love, may have *power,* together with all the saints, to grasp how wide and long and high and deep is the *love* of Christ, and to know this love that surpasses knowledge—that you may be filled to the measure of all the *fullness* of God.

EPHESIANS 3:16–19

$\mathcal{T}$he LORD looks down from heaven . . . to see if there are any who understand, any who seek God.

PSALM 14:2

GLORY IN HIS HOLY NAME; LET THE HEARTS OF THOSE WHO SEEK THE LORD REJOICE. LOOK TO THE LORD AND HIS STRENGTH; SEEK HIS FACE ALWAYS.

1 CHRONICLES 16:10–11

O Jerusalem, Jerusalem . . . how often I have longed to gather your children together, as a hen gathers her chicks under her wings.

Matthew 23:37

$\mathcal{I}$ HAVE BEEN CRUCIFIED WITH CHRIST AND I NO LONGER LIVE, BUT CHRIST LIVES IN ME. THE LIFE I LIVE IN THE BODY, I LIVE BY *faith* IN THE SON OF GOD, WHO *loved* ME AND GAVE HIMSELF FOR ME.

GALATIANS 2:20

In Christ all the fullness of the Deity lives in bodily form, and you have been given fullness in Christ, who is the head over every power and authority.

Colossians 2:9–10

• take me deeper into you • take me deeper into y

*Until we have learned to be
satisfied with fellowship with God,
until he is our rock and our
fortress, we will be restless with
our place in the world.*

ERWIN W. LUTZER

A Woman's Prayer

Dear God of Deliverance,

My life, my world has come to a sudden halt. All that I know, all that makes me feel safe has been suddenly stripped from me. I've lost my bearings—I don't know which way is up and which way is down. My hands tremble, and my knees buckle.

Until this horror came into my life, I felt safe and in control. My life was predictable; my path was mapped out. Now all that's changed.

I think I'd always assumed that pain like this would never come to me. I guess I thought I was immune. But I wasn't. And when it blasted its way into my world, it was like an unexpected punch to the stomach. It took all the wind out of me, and I haven't been able to steady my heart since. I feel so helpless. These events are beyond my control; they seem to be controlling me.

Lord, I seek Your comfort. I seek Your intervention. I need to believe that everything will be OK. I need to feel Your assurance on me. I need to know that You hear me and that You care. What I really want is to be rescued. Please hear me. Please rescue me from this pain.

Your Distressed Child

A Heavenly Promise

Dearest Child,

When you hurt, I hurt too. When you're distressed, I feel your pain.

Even though you're experiencing outward trouble and may feel as if you're wasting away, don't lose heart. For I am renewing you inwardly day by day. I will strengthen your feeble hands; I'll steady your buckling knees. Be strong—don't fear, for I'm your God, and I will save you. Even if you walk through the valley of death, you don't need to fear, for I am with you. I'll guide and protect you as a shepherd does his sheep. I'll command My angels to guard you—they'll hold you in their hands so you won't be harmed.

I will preserve you. I'll stretch out My hand against your foes; I will save you. I am your refuge and strength. I'm always by your side. Even if the whole earth were to give way and the mountains fall into the heart of the sea—even then you need not fear. For I am your light and your salvation, the fortress of your life. Whom shall you fear with Me here to protect you? I am close to the brokenhearted, and I save those whose spirits are crushed.

Your God of Rescue

from Isaiah 63:9; 2 Corinthians 4:16–18; Isaiah 35:3–4; Psalms 23:4; 91:11–12; 138:7; 46:1–3; 27:1; 34:18

Please Rescue Me
God's Word of Promise

We do not *lose* heart. Though
outwardly we are wasting away,
yet inwardly we are being
renewed day by day. For our light
and momentary troubles are
achieving for us an *eternal*
glory that far outweighs them all.
So we *fix* our eyes not on what is
seen, but on what is unseen. For
what is seen is temporary, but
what is *unseen* is eternal.

2 CORINTHIANS 4:16–18

In all their distress he too was distressed, and the angel of his presence saved them. In his love and mercy he redeemed them; he lifted them up and carried them all the days of old.

ISAIAH 63:9

STRENGTHEN THE FEEBLE HANDS, STEADY THE KNEES THAT GIVE WAY; SAY TO THOSE WITH FEARFUL HEARTS, "BE STRONG, DO NOT FEAR; YOUR GOD WILL COME . . . HE WILL COME TO SAVE YOU."

ISAIAH 35:3–4

The LORD is my light and my salvation—whom shall I fear? The LORD is the stronghold of my life—of whom shall I be afraid?

Psalm 27:1

Though I WALK IN THE MIDST OF TROUBLE, YOU *preserve* MY LIFE; YOU STRETCH OUT YOUR HAND AGAINST THE ANGER OF MY FOES, WITH YOUR RIGHT HAND YOU *save* ME.

PSALM 138:7

The LORD is close to the brokenhearted and saves those who are crushed in spirit.

Psalm 34:18

• please rescue me • please rescue me • please rescue

There will come one day a personal and direct touch from God when every tear and perplexity, every oppression and distress, every suffering and pain, and wrong and injustice will have a complete and ample and overwhelming explanation.

OSWALD CHAMBERS

A Woman's Prayer

Dear God of Possibilities,

I come before You hoping and praying that You can work a miracle in my heart. There's a lot about me that needs changing. I'm not talking about minor repairs; I need a complete overhaul. I've tried to change on my own, but it just hasn't worked. Past mistakes haunt me, and present inadequacies chain me to who I am today—not who I want to become.

I want to experience the personal growth I know You've called me to, but I don't know how to get started. Failed efforts have discouraged me, and I find it hard to believe I'll ever make forward progress. I feel powerless to change.

I want the fruit of the Spirit to be in me: love, joy, peace, patience, kindness, goodness, faithfulness, gentleness, and self-control. Those characteristics sound so beautiful but so unlike who I am. I want to "keep in step with the Spirit," as Your Word says in Galatians 5:25. But where do I start?

I seek Your help, Lord. Teach me how to change. I want to be like You.

Your Hopeful Child

A Heavenly Promise

My Precious Child,

I've heard your prayer and will act on your behalf. Whenever you pray according to My will—and your desire to be like Me is definitely according to My will—you can know that you've already received what you have asked of Me.

Your desire for change is the right place to start; now put your desire into action. If you desire to be kind, begin by doing something kind. If you want to be a forgiving person, begin by forgiving someone who has wronged you. If you want to be a loving person, express your love in actions. To attain the characteristics you desire, you must pursue them diligently. You must make every effort to be holy.

Becoming like Me requires that you not conform to the ways of this world but rather be transformed by the renewing of your mind. As your mind is changed, you'll be able to figure out what My will is for your life. As you put your desire into action, you'll see Me do amazing things in you—for I'm able to do immeasurably more than you could ask or imagine. My power and My Word are at work in you this very minute.

Your God of Transformation

from 1 John 5:14–15; 2 Corinthians 8:11; Ephesians 4:32; Colossians 3:12; 1 Thessalonians 5:15; 2 Timothy 2:24; 1 John 3:18; 1 Timothy 6:11; 2 Timothy 2:22; Hebrews 12:14; Romans 12:2; Ephesians 3:20; 1 Thessalonians 2:13

Help Me to Change
God's Word of Promise

Do not *conform* any longer
to the pattern of this world,
but be *transformed* by the
renewing of your mind. Then
you will be able to *test* and
approve what God's will is—his
good, pleasing and *perfect* will.

ROMANS 12:2

*N*ow finish the work, so that your eager willingness to do it may be matched by your completion of it, according to your means.

2 CORINTHIANS 8:11

BE KIND AND COMPASSIONATE TO ONE ANOTHER, FORGIVING EACH OTHER, JUST AS IN CHRIST GOD FORGAVE YOU.

EPHESIANS 4:32

Make every effort to live in peace with all men and to be holy; without holiness no one will see the Lord.

Hebrews 12:14

Pursue RIGHTEOUSNESS, FAITH, *love* AND PEACE, ALONG WITH THOSE WHO CALL ON THE *Lord* OUT OF A PURE HEART.

2 TIMOTHY 2:22

[God] is able to do immeasurably more than all we ask or imagine, according to his power that is at work within us.

Ephesians 3:20

And if we know that he hears us—whatever we ask—we know that we have what we asked of him.

1 John 5:15

• help me to change • help me to change • help r

Keep changing. When you're through changing, you're through.

BRUCE FAIRFIELD BARTON

A Woman's Prayer

Dear Father,

I don't quite know how to say what's on my heart. But if I don't say what's there, I'll never overcome what I'm feeling. The truth is, I'm tired of trying. I'm tired of being nice. I'm tired of being patient. I'm tired of fighting the forces in me that push me away from You. I'm tired of it all.

I'm tempted to just quit! I'm tempted to give in, to give up, to give myself over to the forces I'm resisting.

And yet, Lord, there is a tiny spark in me, a small desire to keep going. The flame is not strong. My will is weak. Still, I do desire to hang on. Instead of giving in to defeat, I want to give myself over to You. But if I'm to make it, if I am to keep going, it must be by Your power and Yours alone.

Hold me together, Lord, for I'm falling apart. Infuse me with Your strength, for I have none of my own.

Your Weary Child

A Heavenly Promise

Dearest Child,

You were right to come to Me with your burden, for I'm gentle with those who seek My help, and I bring rest to weary souls.

In order to tap into My incredible strength, all you must do is come near to Me. When you take just one step toward Me, I'll run to meet you with open arms and a loving heart.

I admonish you, My dear child, to take your eyes off of yourself and your burdens and to put them on your big brother, Jesus. Not only did He come to earth and leave all the glory that was His in heaven, but He endured the painful death of the cross and the separation from Me that came with bearing your sin. Think about Him so you won't grow weary and lose heart.

I never intended for you to bear the heartaches and burdens of this life alone. My eyes are on you; My ears are attentive to your cry. Don't be dismayed, for I am your God. I will strengthen you and help you; I will uphold you with My righteous right hand.

Your God of Strength

from Matthew 11:28–30; James 4:8; Luke 15:20; Hebrews 12:2–4; Psalm 34:15, 17; Isaiah 41:10

I'm Weary of the Struggle
God's Word of Promise

Come to me, all you who are weary and *burdened,* and I will give you rest. Take my yoke upon you and *learn* from me, for I am gentle and humble in heart, and you will find *rest* for your souls. For my yoke is easy and my burden is *light.*

MATTHEW 11:28–30

Come near to God and he will come near to you.

JAMES 4:8

DO NOT FEAR, FOR
I AM WITH YOU; DO
NOT BE DISMAYED,
FOR I AM YOUR GOD.
I WILL STRENGTHEN
YOU AND HELP YOU;
I WILL UPHOLD YOU
WITH MY RIGHTEOUS
RIGHT HAND.

ISAIAH 41:10

Consider him who
endured such opposition
from sinful men, so that
you will not grow
weary and lose heart.
In your struggle against
sin, you have not yet
resisted to the point of
shedding your blood.

Hebrews 12:3–4

Never TIRE OF DOING WHAT IS right.
2 THESSALONIANS 3:13

The eyes of the LORD are on the righteous and his ears are attentive to their cry. . . . The righteous cry out, and the LORD hears them; he delivers them from all their troubles.

Psalm 34:15, 17

• i'm weary of the struggle • i'm weary of the strug

Talk to him in prayer of all your wants, your troubles, even of the weariness you feel in serving him. You cannot speak too freely, too trustfully to him.

FRANÇOIS FENELON

A Woman's Prayer

Dear Father,

I've done it again! I've said something I shouldn't, and I can't unsay it. Sometimes I can hardly believe the things that come out of my mouth. Today I hurt someone I care about very much; at other times I've revealed confidences that were not mine to reveal; and sometimes I say things that are just plain stupid.

Where do these things come from? Sometimes after I've blurted something out, I immediately wish I could pull it right back in. I can't figure out how such words come out of my mouth!

Is there any hope for me? Can I ever learn to control this tongue?

Your Mouthy Child

A Heavenly Promise

Dear Child,

The power of the tongue is amazing, isn't it? It's like fire: one spark can set a whole forest ablaze. Words can wound as surely and swiftly as swords and arrows.

But there is hope. You can learn to control what comes out of your mouth. Start by saying less. The more you talk, the greater your chance of saying something wrong. Remember that I'm in heaven and you're on earth, and let your words be few. Wise people know to hold their tongues. Why, even a fool is thought to be wise if he remains silent!

If you want to clean up your mouth, you must first clean up your heart—for it is out of the overflow of your heart that your mouth speaks.

On the positive side, your words also have great power for good. One kind word can cheer a friend. A gentle response in a heated discussion can soothe angry feelings. The right word spoken at the right time is as beautiful as golden apples in a silver basket.

Be encouraged, for as My Spirit continues to have His way in you, the results will be love, joy, peace, patience, kindness, goodness, faithfulness, gentleness, and self-control.

Your Loving Father
from James 3:5–6; Psalm 64:3; Ecclesiastes 5:2; Proverbs 10:19; 17:28; Luke 6:45; Proverbs 12:25; 15:1; 25:11; 15:23; Galatians 5:22–23

I Say Things I Shouldn't
God's Word of Promise

The tongue is a small part of the body, but it makes great *boasts*. Consider what a great forest is set on fire by a small spark. The tongue also is a *fire*, a world of evil among the parts of the body. It *corrupts* the whole person, sets the whole course of his life on fire, and is itself set on fire by hell.

JAMES 3:5–6

*D*o not be quick with your mouth, do not be hasty in your heart to utter anything before God. God is in heaven and you are on earth, so let your words be few.

ECCLESIASTES 5:2

The good man brings good things out of the good stored up in his heart, and the evil man brings evil things out of the evil stored up in his heart. For out of the overflow of his heart his mouth speaks.

Luke 6:45

WHEN WORDS ARE MANY, SIN IS NOT ABSENT, BUT HE WHO HOLDS HIS TONGUE IS WISE.

PROVERBS 10:19

A WORD APTLY SPOKEN IS LIKE APPLES OF *gold* IN SETTINGS OF SILVER.

PROVERBS 25:11

An anxious heart weighs a man down, but a kind word cheers him up.

Proverbs 12:25

Even a fool is thought wise if he keeps silent, and discerning if he holds his tongue.

Proverbs 17:28

• i say things i shouldn't • i say things i should

*Kind words can be short
and easy to speak but their
echoes are truly endless.*

MOTHER TERESA

A Woman's Prayer

Dear Father,

What a gracious, loving God You are! Today my heart is overflowing with Your joy—a joy that springs from deep inside me, a joy that is founded in You. So often I come to You burdened or asking for help. And I know You're happy to hear me no matter why I come—but today I want to celebrate Your deep, abiding joy.

Looking back at my life, I see Your blessings at every turn. Though I've had my share of difficulties, You were always with me. Your light is constantly shining, even in the blackest night. And I've observed a comforting truth as You've walked with me day by day: It's Your strength that fills me with joy. When I feel weak and inadequate, I turn to You for help; and as You supply me with Your strength, joy floods my soul.

Thank You for creating in me a joy that is not limited by happiness. I can be in the most unhappy circumstances, yet be confident and comforted by Your ever-present joy. Along with all of creation, I praise You for Your abiding presence.

Your Joyful Child

Dear Joyful Child,

How pleased I am that you're learning the true meaning and source of joy. As you take My Word into your heart, My teachings will be a constant source of joy to you, and your eyes will sparkle with my light. If you obey My commands, you will remain in My love, and your joy will be complete.

My joy stored up in your heart will make you strong, for My joy is your strength. Your heart will leap for joy as you trust in Me and lean on My strength. You can be confident that My light shines even in your darkest troubles and that even the night will shine like the day, for darkness is like light to Me.

Just look around, and you'll see that all of nature joins you in your joy. The rivers clap their hands, and the mountains sing. The fields are jubilant, and the trees of the forest sing for joy. When I comfort you, the heavens shout for joy and the earth rejoices. Because I have forgiven your sins and swept away your offenses like a cloud, the mountains burst into song.

Because you live your life for Me, all your tomorrows carry the promise of My deep, abiding joy.

Your God of Everlasting Joy

from Psalm 19:8; John 15:10–11; Nehemiah 8:10; Psalms 28:7; 18:28; 139:11–12; 98:8; 96:12; Isaiah 49:13; 44:22–23; Proverbs 10:28

Fill Me with Your Joy
God's Word of Promise

"I have *swept* away your offenses like a cloud, your sins like the morning mist. Return to me, for I have *redeemed* you." Sing for joy, O heavens, for the LORD has done this; *shout* aloud, O earth beneath. Burst into song, you mountains, you forests and all your trees.

ISAIAH 44:22–23

*T*hose who sow in tears will reap with songs of joy. He who goes out weeping, carrying seed to sow, will return with songs of joy, carrying sheaves with him.

PSALM 126:5–6

SHOUT FOR JOY, O HEAVENS; REJOICE, O EARTH; BURST INTO SONG, O MOUNTAINS! FOR THE LORD COMFORTS HIS PEOPLE AND WILL HAVE COMPASSION ON HIS AFFLICTED ONES.

ISAIAH 49:13

The precepts of the LORD are right, giving joy to the heart. The commands of the LORD are radiant, giving light to the eyes.

Psalm 19:8

The JOY OF THE LORD IS *your* STRENGTH.

NEHEMIAH 8:10

The LORD is my strength and my shield; my heart trusts in him, and I am helped. My heart leaps for joy and I will give thanks to him in song.

Psalm 28:7

*Joy is the echo of
God's life within us.*

JOSEPH COLUMBA MARMION

• fill me with your joy • fill me with your joy • fill me

DATE _____

_____

_____

_____

_____

_____

_____

_____

_____

_____

_____

_____

_____

_____

_____

_____

_____

_____

_____

_____

_____

_____

_____

_____

DATE _____

_____

_____

_____

_____

_____

_____

_____

_____

_____

_____

_____

_____

_____

_____

_____

_____

_____

_____

_____

_____

_____

_____

_____

DATE

_____

_____

_____

_____

_____

_____

_____

_____

_____

_____

_____

_____

_____

_____

_____

_____

_____

_____

_____

_____

_____

_____

_____